Adjutant General's Office New York

Proceedings Attending the Presentation of Regimental

Colors

To the Legislature, April 20, 1864

Adjutant General's Office New York

Proceedings Attending the Presentation of Regimental Colors
To the Legislature, April 20, 1864

ISBN/EAN: 9783744729574

Printed in Europe, USA, Canada, Australia, Japan

Cover: Foto ©ninafisch / pixelio.de

More available books at **www.hansebooks.com**

EXCELSIOR.

TROPHY FLAGS.

State of New York.

— •◆•◆• —

PROCEEDINGS ATTENDING THE PRESENTATION

OF

REGIMENTAL COLORS

TO THE LEGISLATURE,

April 20, 1864.

ALBANY:
VAN BENTHUYSEN'S STEAM PRINTING HOUSE.
1864.

THIS WORK IS DEDICATED

TO THE

VOLUNTEER TROOPS FROM THE STATE OF NEW YORK,

IN

TESTIMONY OF THEIR DEVOTION

TO OUR

COMMON COUNTRY.

JOHN T. SPRAGUE, *Adjutant General.*

HEAD QUARTERS STATE OF NEW YORK, }
   Albany, N. Y., *June 20, 1864.* }

HIS EXCELLENCY

HORATIO SEYMOUR,

GOVERNOR,

COMMANDER-IN-CHIEF OF THE STATE OF NEW YORK.

STAFF:

ADJUTANT GENERAL,
Brig. Gen. JOHN T. SPRAGUE,
(Lt. Col. 11th Infantry U. S. Army.)

INSPECTOR GENERAL,
Brig. Gen. JOSIAH T. MILLER.

ENGINEER-IN-CHIEF,
Brig. Gen. ISAAC VANDERPOEL.

JUDGE ADVOCATE GENERAL,
Brig. Gen. NELSON T. WATERBURY.

SURGEON GENERAL,
Brig. Gen. JOHN V. P. QUACKENBUSH.

QUARTERMASTER GENERAL,
Brig. Gen. S. VISSCHER TALCOTT.

PAYMASTER GENERAL,
Col. JOHN D. VAN BUREN.

AID-DE-CAMP,
Col. B. TIBBITS.

MILITARY SECRETARY,
Maj. WILLIAM KIDD.

Albany, June 1, 1864.

PROCEEDINGS

IN REGARD TO THE

PRESENTATION OF REGIMENTAL FLAGS.

———••———

IN ASSEMBLY, WEDNESDAY, *April 13, 1864.*

By unanimous consent, on motion of MR. CROOKE,

Resolved (if the Senate concur), That the Senate and Assembly will meet at this Chamber on Wednesday evening, 20th inst., at 7 o'clock, to receive the flags of volunteer regiments of this State.

MR. CROOKE moved that a session of the House be held on Wednesday evening for that purpose.

MR. SPEAKER put the question, whether the House would agree to said motion, and it was determined in the affirmative.

Returned from Senate April 15th, with notice of concurrence.

BUREAU OF MILITARY STATISTICS.

The Legislature in 1863, made provision for an office, whose particular business it should be to collect for preservation and future historical use, the records and statistics which should tend to illustrate the action of the people of the State of New York in the present war. These inquiries embraced biographies of officers and men, the history of regiments, and the action of towns, counties and cities, having reference to the raising of men or means for the war, or the support of families of volunteers.

The Laws of 1864 (Chapter 51), made further provision for continuing the Bureau of Military Statistics, and for greatly extending its facilities.

A part of its duties related to the custody of the flags of regiments whose term of service had expired, and those colors which from wear and injury were of no further use in the field. Of these, nearly one hundred have now been collected, and it is believed that ultimately the greater part of these honored memorials of the valor and patriotism of New York troops, will be gathered into this repository.

On the 23d of April, 1863, seven regimental flags, which had been returned to the State, were presented to the Governor, in the presence of the Legislature, with impressive ceremonies.

The intention of the State Government in adopting these measures, was mainly to express to the world, and to place upon record in the most solemn and eloquent manner, their high appreciation of the services of its troops in the field, and to convey to such as might then or thereafter be engaged in the service, an assurance that their patriotism and valor were known and approved. While resting assured that these troops would do or omit nothing that should dishonor themselves or the State, it was deemed proper to bring prominently before their minds the important truth, that their conduct was under observation, and that their victories were a subject of gratification and pride to the State. A

motive was thus added for winning new laurels
in the campaign, and of adding a new lustre to
their fame. Every soldier might feel that upon
himself depended in some degree the reputation
and honor of the Empire State, and that his
personal character was pledged in their maintenance and defence.

During the year 1863, and early months of
1864, many flags were added to the collections
of the Bureau of Military Statistics, and of these
fifty that had been borne by regiments and
batteries in the field, were presented by the
Governor to the Legislature, convened for that
occasion, in the Assembly Chamber, on the
evening of April 20th, 1864. To the proceedings upon that occasion, and to the history of
the flags then presented, the present work is
devoted.

The Bureau of Military Statistics is now
authorized to receive worn out flags from organ-
izations still in the service, in exchange for new.
The law provides that requisitions for new flags
claimed under this act, shall be made by the
commanding officers of regiments upon the Quar-

2

ter Master General, and that they shall be accompanied by a certificate of the Chief of the Bureau of Military Statistics, that the old flag with its accompanying history has been deposited in his office.

The Bureau is also forming a museum of articles of military interest connected with the present war, and arrangements are being made for the preservation of its collections against chance of accident, and for their public display.

As extensive a collection as possible is being made of biographical notices, journals and narratives, published documents, correspondence and original papers. These will be carefully kept for future reference and use, under such regulations as may be deemed necessary for their safety. Such photographic or other portraits of officers or privates, as may be contributed to the collection, will be indexed and bound, or otherwise preserved.

The active co-operation of officers and soldiers now or formerly in the public service, is solicited in increasing the collections already begun. The united efforts of our citizens may it is hoped,

form a collection that will acquire interest and
value commensurate with the magnitude and
importance of the subject, and present a lasting
evidence of the patriotic efforts of the people of
New York in the preservation of the Union, in
the present great national crisis.

All communications or donations intended for
this purpose, should be addressed to

Col. LOCKWOOD L. DOTY,

Chief of Bureau of Military Statistics,

Albany, N. Y.

PROCEEDINGS ON PRESENTATION OF FLAGS.

The Assembly met at the appointed hour, and being called to order, committees were appointed to wait upon the Governor, Lieutenant Governor, Adjutant General, and Senate, to notify them that they were in readiness to receive them.

The Senate having arrived, were seated in front of the Speaker's desk. The flags were then brought in, each one being borne by a young gentleman who volunteered for the occasion, and arranged in a double line along the middle aisle of the Assembly Chamber.

The Governor, Adjutant General and Military Staff, accompanied by the Assembly Committees, consisting of GEN. CROOKE, COL. BULLOCK, CAPT. FILKINS, CAPT. OSWALD and CAPT. PARKER, then came in and took their places, the Governor in the Chair presiding, with the Speaker of the Assembly on his right.

A large number of citizens and ladies were present, and a band of music was in attendance.

After the convention had been called to order, Adjutant General SPRAGUE arose and delivered the following address:

"'In Rama there was a voice heard; lamentation, and weeping, and great moaning: Rachel weeping for her children, and would not be comforted because they are not.'

"To-night there is a voice coming up to us throughout this land, reverberating within these walls with fearful emphasis and melancholy cadence, breaking upon the hearts of many now within the sound of my voice: it is the wail of America weeping for her children.

"It is meet for us to be here to-night, my countrymen, and may we, like the patriarch of old, come up high upon Mount Horeb to worship. Here let us burn incense upon the altar of our country, and may the smoke of the sacrifice rise above these venerated walls, surmounting the hills around us, and settle down upon every heart in our distracted land.

"Why this forest of banners here to-night?—

spectres of bloody battle-fields; cerements of
the grave; fit garments for brave men. It is
because our country is rent by a civil war. Every
one of these have a tale of fearful and eventful
interest, of joy and sorrow, of glory and renown.

" Those stars, now dimmed by the sulphurous
smoke of the battle-field, once glittered and
shone forth from many a secluded hamlet, from
true and patriotic hearts throughout the State.
Those stripes once shot forth like the radiance
of a morning's sun, from cities, villages and
associations, until they coruscated into the
expressive banner of our country; while the
dark eagle — emblematic of our greatness and
power — soared aloft and swept its way to the
battle-field, amid the universal shouts of a patriotic and indignant people. Many a father gave
a hearty farewell to his only son, as the tears
coursed down the gorges of his manly cheek.
Mothers clasped to their bosoms the support of
their declining years, and bade God speed them
to the battle-field. Wives clung tenaciously to
the companions of their lives, while the house-
hold extended their tiny hands to bid a last fare-

well. She whose heart swelled with fervor and affection in 'love's young dream,' tore asunder the cords that bound her, and with pride and enthusiasm saw in him the brave defender of her country's honor.

" The shifting scenes of the drama have passed before us, and these banners have returned to narrate with graphic power, tales of sorrow and trials, as well as of fidelity, patriotism and renown. The eagle spreads his dark plumage o'ershadowing us with sadness, and perches upon many a solitary threshold within the limits of this State. Such a representation as we have here to-night, comes home to us with many salutary lessons of instruction.

" It grapples with our hearts, arouses our sensibilities, awakens within us sober reflection, and bewilders the mind, when we attempt to withdraw the veil obscuring the future, and the cry involuntary comes forth, how long! Oh, how long shall our country be rent by a civil war!

" It is better for us to-night to be in the house of mourning than in the house of feasting. This is a time for serious reflection, when we should look at facts and events without disguise. In this terrible conflict now raging for the restoration of our country, the crisis has come. We are to conquer or be conquered. Our destiny is to restore the power of our country, the supremacy of our rights and our laws, our Constitution and the Union. If we fail in this, the iron yoke of bondage is upon us, and we become a by-word and a reproach to the civilized world.

"The fearful passions of revenge will ravage our land, and our hearthstones will be made desolate with fire and with blood. Your hoarded wealth will be turned to cinders, and your gold to dross. This war can only be terminated by the power, by the energy and fidelity of the people. Blood and treasure must be staked, which, with a wise, sagacious, and charitable statesmanship, our country will be restored. Men of all classes must come up to the work without partisan or fanatical zeal, and with pure and patriotic sentiments. Personal and political feelings must be subdued; and whatever may be the difference of opinion, accord to each, in charity, integrity and fidelity, in maintaining the power and supremacy of our country. Maintain our Government; give to its measures a cordial support; and if successful, it will meet a corresponding reward. If otherwise, punishment will ensue from the condemnation of the world. It is the people who control; look to it with care, wisdom and caution. In my opinion this war has but commenced; one part of the country is a battlefield where homes are desolated and wives and children are seeking shelter and food. Here, in our midst, extravagance, plethoric wealth, joy and carelessness prevail, and thousands are hoarding treasure gleaned from the blood of our countrymen. The rich man plies the measure of his demands as embarrassments increase, wrung from the daily toil of the soldier, the citizen, and the poor who earn their daily bread by the sweat of their brow.

"Our streets are thronged by young and hearty men, as money keeps them from the conflict of arms. Money — gold — has become the representative of patriotism. That pure and genial flame that was ignited in the hearts of our forefathers, securing to us the institutions we so long

3

enjoyed, has become dimmed; it is a phosphoric
light that glitters, but is cold.

"Being so far removed from the conflicts
which we have observed for three years past, we
have not realized the revenge and vindictive-
ness of the enemy. The strife is now in the
midst of us, around us, and before us. We have
been made the instruments in the hands of a
wise Providence, for the accomplishment of some
great end, or for our punishment as a nation.
Our course has been one of vain boasting, and
self-reliance, not with penitential reverence for
the blessings received. Patriotism is a reli-
gion allied to our God. Without it, pure and
unaffected, no nation can be saved. This pic-
ture may not be acceptable, but they are facts —
unmistakable facts, and we should meet them
like men. Let us draw lessons of instruction
from the past, and look with courage and confidence to the future, keeping steadily in view the
motto — 'conquer or be conquered.'

"With all this we have much to be proud of in
the events which have transpired during the past
three years. The soldier is well cared for. The

United States Hospital Department is perfect in its details, and administered with vigor and liberality by its efficient officers. Upwards of a million and a half of dollars have been raised by Military Fairs in this State. The Sanitary and Christian Commission have been untiring in their zeal and devotion. The State has a depot for the soldier in the city of New York, in which twenty-seven thousand men have been made comfortable and happy during the past year. Our armies have been victorious, and the ranks are being filled by patriotic and devoted men. Crushing this rebellion and restoring our country, is but a question of time.

"This State has sent to the field 293,000 men, and it would be strange, indeed, if there should not be mingled in their experience, much that is sorrowful, as well as the pride and glory surrounding achievements.

"These banners come back to us without reproach. There are now in the field upwards of one hundred and thirty thousand men from this State. Should occasion require, more are prepared to go.

" From the records now before me, which I shall read, there is enough to cause every citizen to be proud of his native State, and to cause a feeling of gratitude and of pride, that 'Excelsior' can be inscribed upon her banners without reproach.

*   *   *   *   *   *

"My task is done. As your representative, and on behalf of those brave men now in the field, and in the presence of both Houses of the Legislature, I deposit these colors in the Statistical Bureau of this State, and it is to be hoped that not a long time may elapse before an appropriate building will be erected where they can be displayed in all time to come. There let the breezes of Heaven blow gently on their gaping wounds, amid the smiles and caresses of a free, intelligent, loyal and happy people.

"The ivy may cling its tendrils around the sturdy oak, but the parent trunk must die.

" The moss of ages may gather upon mouldering stones, broken columns, and the architecture of the age; but the memory of these defenders of our country will live in a perennial green, and their names will be inscribed in letters of eternal and living light upon the escutcheon of their country.

"Spirits of the departed brave, if you are permitted to look down upon our devotions here to-night, assemble around the immortal Washington, and hear the accents of a grateful people. Peace! Peace! we will watch with pious care the laurels that shade your urns, and wear your names engraven upon our hearts."

The flags were then brought forward by regiments in their numerical order, and the history of each was read by the Adjutant General, as hereinafter given.

Mr. Alvord, the Speaker of the Assembly, then arose and made the following remarks:

"Unprepared on this occasion, from the circumstances which surround this period of time, yet at the request of those gathered together here, I shall say a few words to you. It is with mingled feelings of sad solemnity and joyousness that I do address you — a solemnity which has been impressed upon me by the words of the distinguished gentleman who has this night, in

the name of the regiments, presented these flags
to take their place in the archives of the State.
For he has spoken of troublous times which these
flags have seen — of the blood, the slaughter,
and the dead which have marked their pathway
in the battles which have raged around them as
they have been borne forth in the conflict; but,
at the same time, with a joyous and buoyant
feeling, I welcome these flags home again to
their native soil of the State of New York, for
it shows that her sons have fought nobly and
well in this struggle for her country's good and
for her maintenance and her perpetuity. We
are fighting a battle in which we have got to
conquer or die. We are fighting a battle in
which is to be established for all time that God
has written in the decrees of Heaven that man
is to work it out upon earth that he is capable of
self-government, and that we shall in the end be
free. Many of these flags have been borne forth
by regiments who, to-day, with a more firm step
than when they first went forth, are now press-
ing upon the last recesses of the enemies of our
country.

"Aye, and I tell you that out of the remnants and battles which are here shown to you, there will come up a brighter and nobler banner in the future — our stars will be increased in multitude — our stripes will float over a free and happy people from one end of the country to the other. And welcome are these flags to the archives of our State, for each and every one of them is a page in its history. And I welcome them for another reason. Partizan feeling and party strifes sink into insignificance before them, for the blood of all of us has mingled in this strife — there has been no distinction — brothers have stood shoulder to shoulder with brothers, and exposed their lives to overcome the enemies of their country. I trust that these banners will bind around us the silken chains of concord and unity. I know that whatever may be our bickerings here, when the time shall come, if it must needs come, it will be the one universal thought and action upon the part of the people of the North to fight on and fight ever, until the banner of our country, undimmed of any stars, and with no stripes removed from it, shall float free over

the land, from Maine to the Gulf, from the
Atlantic to the Pacific. I thank you for having
thus far listened to me. I have nothing further
to say, except to introduce to you upon this occasion, as the presiding officer of this assemblage,
one whose eloquence needs no eulogium from my
tongue, and whose heart beats as warmly and as
honestly for the Union as that of any among us."

His Excellency, Governor SEYMOUR, arose and
addressed the assemblage as follows:

"With a wise and patriotic liberality, this State
has provided that the history of every regiment
it has sent to the war shall be preserved, and
that there shall be a place where shall be deposited the banners which they have borne in the
contests in which they have been engaged. I
am sure that the heart of every man within the
sound of my voice, has been moved this night,
when he has seen these banners brought back
again into our State, so sad, and yet so glorious.

"Every one has been proud of our State,
when we heard from the lips of General Sprague,
from whence these banners went. That some
were sent from the Great Metropolis, some from

the shores of our great lakes, others from the
shores of Lake Champlain, and others again from
the valleys of the Mohawk, the Delaware, the
Susquehanna, or the Allegany. From whatever
part of our State they have gone, they went
from sections that had already a glorious history.
The whole history of New York, from its beginning to this day, has been an honorable one. It
has required no stretch of imagination to pic-
ture to ourselves the scene when these brave,
bold and stalwart men went forth from the hills
and valleys and cities of our land to battle for
our flag. You have seen them from time to time,
returning here shattered and broken, the mere
remnants of those glorious bands, which excited
our admiration and our enthusiasm on their
departure. And in their history you have an
epitome of the whole war. The banners that
have been presented to you this night have been
fanned by the breezes of Carolina, have been
dampened with the dews that have fallen in the
swamps of Virginia, have drooped under the
almost tropical sun of Louisiana, have floated
high in the heavens 'in the battle above the

4

clouds,' at Lookout Mountain, where, under their
folds, we won an honorable victory. It is well
that our State on this occasion has shown its
ancient fidelity to the flag of our country, to the
Union of these States, and to the Constitution
of our land. It is fit and becoming that this
great State, on whose soil this flag of ours was
first given to the breezes of Heaven, and which
was first displayed in defence of the very spot
on which we now stand, shall be foremost in its
defence. The State of New York has nearly
130,000 men in the field. During the whole of
this contest, it has furnished one-fifth of our
armies. I believe I may say that her sons have
been inferior to none in their bravery, their
devotion, their courage or their patriotism.

"I will not attempt to add to the emotions
you have felt upon the display of these flags. I
have no eloquence which shall compare with that
of these mute emblems, whose very rags and
tatters are made glorious with the memories and
histories of martial achievements. I have only
to add a fervent prayer that all the sacrifices that
have been made, that the blood which has been

poured forth, may not have been made and shed
in vain. May Almighty God, in his providence,
grant that all these things may tend to the wel-
fare, the glory, and the honor of this land of ours.
In the midst of the darkness which now over-
hangs us, in view of the uncertainties of the
contest, with the full knowledge that still further
life must be rendered up, and still more blood be
shed for the cause in which we are engaged,
placing full reliance upon a wisdom greater than
man's wisdom, and trusting in a goodness and
a mercy far superior to that which can actuate
the human breast, we hope that these sacrifices
may end in our country's glory and honor. I
receive, on behalf of the great State, whose
Chief Magistrate I am, these emblems of the
valor and the patriotism of our sons. They will
be set aside and preserved, monuments of the
devotion of our people in the struggle for the
success and glory of our common country."

GEN. CROOKE responded:

"He said the main reason for his consenting
to speak, was to speak with reference to his own
locality. The reason why Long Island had no

representative among the flags was, that they
felt so proud of their trophies, that they would
not let them be taken from Brooklyn. They
preferred to keep them there. He was glad that
mention had been made of the militia. He was
proud of the militia. He referred to the 14th
Brooklyn regiment, which rejoiced in being
called the Militia of the Army of the Potomac.
The militia did amount to something, and it had
sometimes been said that he had ' militia on the
brain.' Let it be so understood. He was ready
to make sacrifices for that branch of the service.
To a great extent, the militia of the State owed
its efficiency to Governor SEYMOUR.

"The Governor had done much to aid in the
organization, and it was proper that he should
have credit. He felt more sanguine of the result
of the contest in which we are engaged than
GEN. SPRAGUE had expressed. He did not feel
despondent. He could not but feel that the
result would be successful and glorious, and he
presumed he should think so if the war was
to continue for ten years to come. He believed the ladies sympathized with him in this

opinion, for they always had confidence in good results."

The following lines, written by ALFRED B. STREET, State Librarian, were prepared for the occasion:

Aye, bring back the banners and fold them in rest!
They have wrought their high mission, their holy behest!
Stained with blood, scorched with flame, hanging tattered and
    torn,
Yet dearer, by far, than when, bright, they were borne
      By brave hearts to glory!

As we gaze at their tatters, what battle-fields rise,
Fields flashing in deeds of sublimest emprise?
When earth rocked with thunder, the sky glared with fire,
And Havoc's red pinion dashed onward in ire!
      Deeds deathless in glory!

Press the stars to the lips, clasp the stripes to the heart!
Let us swear their grand memories shall not depart!
They have waved in this contest of Freedom and Right,
And our Eagle shall waft them, wide streaming in light,
      To our summit of glory!

There — hope darting beacons, starred shrines — shall they
    glow,
Lighting Liberty's way to the breast of the foe; —
Till her spear smites with splendor the gloom, and our sun,
One broad central orb, shall again brighten one
      Mighty nation of glory!

The ceremonies of the evening being completed, the Governor and Senate withdrew, and the Speaker declared the House adjourned to the stated hour for business on the following day.

COLORS OF THE 10TH REGIMENT N. Y. S. V.

(One Flag.)

This flag was presented by the city of New York, on the departure of the 10th regiment to the seat of war.

It was the first American flag raised over the Custom House at Norfolk, Va., after its recovery by Union troops, and was borne in the SEVEN DAYS BEFORE RICHMOND, 2D BULL RUN, ANTIETAM and FREDERICKSBURGH. At the latter place it was shot from the hands of the bearer. Several of the guard were killed under it. The 10th regiment left a battalion of four companies that has since been increased to six, in the field, upon the return of the main body at the expiration of its two years term. The flag is transmitted to the State Archives by MAJOR GEO. F. HOOPER.

COLORS OF THE 12TH REGIMENT N. Y. S. V.

(One Flag.)

This regiment was organized at Syracuse, although Constantia, Batavia and Homer each furnished a company. At Syracuse, upon leaving for the seat of war (May 2d, 1861), the ladies presented this flag, which has been carried through every service in which it has been engaged. At the expiration of two years, the regiment returned, and the flag was placed in the custody of the State.

The 12th regiment was engaged in the battle of BLACKBURN'S FORD, and at Bull Run was in reserve. After spending many months building and guarding forts in front of Washington, it was sent to the Peninsula, where it was engaged in the SEIGE OF YORKTOWN, and the battles of HANOVER COURT HOUSE, GAINES' MILL, SAVAGE'S STATION, WHITE OAK SWAMP and MALVERN HILL.

Returning to the front of Washington, it participated in the SECOND BATTLE OF BULL RUN, and afterwards in the campaign in Maryland, and the battle of FREDERICKSBURGH. It was during the period of active field service, a part of the 3d Brigade, 1st Division of the 5th Army Corps.

COLORS OF THE 13TH REGIMENT N. Y. S. V.

(Three Flags.)

Three flags, two the National colors and one an embroidered banner, have been returned by the 13th regiment to the custody of the State for preservation.

The regimental banner was presented by the ladies of Rochester.

The new National flag was carried in the first battle of BULL RUN only. The holes in the union were made upon that occasion.

The old National flag was carried habitually on the march and in action.

The 13th regiment was raised in Rochester, under Colonel, now General ISAAC QUIMBY, in April, 1861, and with the 12th N. Y. Volunteers, were the first troops to pass through Baltimore after the riot of April 19th, and the attack upon the 6th Massachusetts regiment. It participated

in the FIRST BATTLE OF BULL RUN, SEIGE OF YORK-
TOWN, battles of HANOVER COURT HOUSE, MECHAN-
ICSVILLE, GAINES' MILL, TURKEY BEND, MALVERN
HILL, SECOND BULL RUN, ANTIETAM (in reserve),
SHEPARDSTOWN, and FREDERICKSBURGH. The regi-
ment, after an honorable service of two years,
was mustered out on the 14th of May, 1863.
The flags are transmitted to the Bureau of Mili-
tary Statistics, by COL. E. G. MARSHALL.

COLORS OF THE 14TH REGIMENT N. Y. S. V.

(One Flag.)

This regiment was organized at Albany, from companies raised in Utica, Rome, Boonville, Batavia, Lowville and Hudson. It joined the army of the Potomac in June, 1861, and was engaged in the SEIGE OF YORKTOWN, and in the battles of NEW BRIDGE, HANOVER COURT HOUSE, MECHANICSVILLE, GAINES' MILL, MALVERN HILL, SECOND BULL RUN, SHEPARDSTOWN, FREDERICKSBURGH and CHANCELLORSVILLE.

The 14th regiment received this banner from the hand of Governor MORGAN, on its departure for the field, and on the expiration of its term of enlistment, it was returned to Governor SEYMOUR soiled and tattered, but not dishonored. In reporting the history of the regiment, it is added with commendable pride that *the 14th never had its pickets driven in, and never turned its back to the enemy in battle.*

COLORS OF THE 16TH REGIMENT N. Y. S. V.

(Two Flags.)

These flags were presented by MRS. JOSEPH HOWLAND of Fishkill, N. Y., the banner in June, 1861, and the National flag, at Camp Franklin, near Alexandria, in March, 1862, when COL. HOWLAND assumed command of the regiment. These flags have been borne in eighteen battles, skirmishes and reconnoisances, the principal of which were WEST POINT, Va., GAINES' MILL, and the six following days of fighting and marching; CRAMPTON GAP, ANTIETAM, 1st and 2d FREDE-RICKSBURGH. At Gaines' Mill the Color Bearers were three times shot down, and every one of the Color Guard was either killed or wounded except one. The staff of the regimental flag was struck by a ball, while in the hands of the Color Bearer, and the ferule indented so that it could not be moved on the staff. At Crampton

Gap, Corp. Charles H. Conant was instantly killed by a Minnie ball through the head while holding one of the flags, and Corp. Robert Watson of the Color Guard, was shot through the leg. In this action the regiment, in charging upon the enemy, captured a rebel battle-flag from an Alabama regiment.

Upon the expiration of its term of two years, the 16th regiment returned with its colors, which were presented to his Excellency, the Governor, to be deposited in the Bureau of Military Statistics, the pledge given by the regiment to the donor, to "stand by, defend and preserve them," having been faithfully and honorably redeemed.

COLORS OF THE 17TH REGIMENT N. Y. S. V.

(Three Flags.)

One National flag and two banners have been returned by this regiment.

The National flag, much worn, was presented to the regiment by eight lady friends of COL. LANSING, and the blue banner by the city of New York. This regiment, sometimes known as the "Westchester Chasseurs," was organized in New York, and participated in the SEIGE OF YORKTOWN, and battles of HANOVER COURT HOUSE (where it captured the first cannon taken from the enemy by the army of the Potomac), GROVETON (where it lost 13 officers and 250 men, killed and wounded), ANTIETAM, FREDERICKSBURGH and CHAN-CELLORSVILLE.

The 17th regiment was brigaded with the 3d Brigade, 1st Division, 5th Army Corps, and its two years term of service expired in the spring

of 1863.   A veteran regiment made up in part
of men who served in this command, is now in
the field, and is serving in the Department of
the Southwest.

COLORS OF THE 18TH REGIMENT N. Y. S. V.

(One Flag.)

This flag was presented to the 18th regiment, COL. WM. A. JACKSON, by his lady friends of Albany, June 1, 1861, shortly before departure for the field. It bears the inscription "Rally around them."

This regiment was organized at Albany, from companies enlisted in Albany, Schenectady, Fishkill, Walkill, Middletown and Ogdensburgh. It was engaged in the battles of FIRST BULL RUN, WEST POINT, GAINES' MILL, CHARLES CITY CROSS ROADS, MALVERN HILL, CRAMPTON PASS, ANTIETAM, FIRST AND SECOND FREDERICKSBURGH, and CHANCEL-LORSVILLE. Upon the expiration of the term of enlistment, this regiment returned home, and the colors were placed in the custody of the State by COL. GEO. R. MYERS, the last Colonel, who led the regiment in all its services after leaving the Peninsula, in August, 1862.

6

COLORS OF THE 24TH REGIMENT N. Y. S. V.

(One Flag.)

———— •• ————

This regiment was organized at Oswego, and was mostly enlisted in that county. It entered the field in 1861; served during the active campaign of 1862, and upon its returning after two years' service, placed this flag in the State archives. It is inscribed with its own history: Upon one side " FALMOUTH, RAPPAHANNOCK STATION, WARRENTON SPRINGS, GAINESVILLE, GROVETON, 2d BULL RUN, SOUTH MOUNTAIN, ANTIETAM, FREDERICKSBURGH, RAPPAHANNOCK CROSSING, CHANCELLORSVILLE," and upon the other: "24th REGIMENT, IRON BRIGADE, 1st DIVISION, 1st ARMY CORPS."

COLORS OF THE 26TH REGIMENT N. Y. S. V.

(One Flag.)

This regiment was organized at Elmira, from companies raised in Utica, Hamilton, Rochester and Tioga county. It served in the campaign of Virginia, under GEN. POPE; and in Maryland, under McCLELLAN; followed the enemy as he retired into Virginia, and returned at the expiration of its two years term of service. This flag was transmitted to the State archives, with the following letter:

"To GEN. J. T. SPRAGUE,
ADJUTANT GENERAL, N. Y.

"SIR: I have the honor to return to the custody of the State of New York, the colors carried by this regiment since June, 1861. They have been borne through every battle of Eastern Virginia, and under their folds have fallen five good and true men.   *   *   *   *   *

We return them to the State from which we

received them, well knowing they will be cherished as mementoes of the living and the dead. They bear the marks of bullets, and of the blood of those who defended them, and, as such, will always be regarded with respect and veneration by those who are left to mourn the loss of their comrades on the field of battle.

Very respectfully,

Your obedient servant,

R. H. RICHARDSON,

Col. Commanding 26*th N. Y. Vols.*

This regiment was at the battles of CEDAR MOUNTAIN, RAPPAHANNOCK STATION, THOROUGHFARE GAP, GROVETON, SOUTH MOUNTAIN, ANTIETAM, FREDERICKSBURGH and CHANCELLORSVILLE.

At Groveton, about 150 were killed and wounded; at Antietam, 30; and at Fredericksburgh, 162.

COLORS OF THE 27TH REGIMENT N. Y. S. V.

(One Flag.)

This regiment was organized at Elmira, from companies raised in Rochester, Binghamton, Lyons, Angelica and Lima, and entered the field under Col. SLOCUM, since promoted to the rank of Major General in command of a corps. Col. BARTLETT, who succeeded, was also promoted to the command of a division.

The 27th regiment received this flag, May 22d, 1861, from Company G., and this company the same day received it from Mrs. PHILIP CHURCH of Belvidere. It was borne in the battles of 1st BULL RUN, MECHANICSVILLE, WEST POINT, GAINES' MILL, GOLDSBOROUGH'S FARM, CHICKAHOMINY, WHITE OAK CREEK, MALVERN HILL, CRAMPTON PASS, ANTIETAM, and the 1st and 2d battles of FREDERICKSBURGH. The bearer at Gaines' Mill was severely wounded. The flag has been many times struck

by the enemy's shot, and the larger holes were
made by fragments of shell.

The star in the case appended to the lance,
was literally shot out of the flag, while the regiment was storming the Heights of Fredericksburgh, in May, 1863. It was contributed to the
Bureau of Military Statistics by A. L. VAN NESS,
of Dansville, N. Y., who was the Color Bearer in
that assault. The flag itself was transmitted by
COL. ADAMS.

GUIDON OF THE 28TH REGIMENT N. Y. S. V.

(One Flag.)

—— ◆◆ ——

At the battle of Chancellorsville, JOHN OTTO SWAN of Medina, aged 15 years (enlisted as a drummer, and then acting as a marker), displayed great activity and energy. A soldier of Company E was shot dead, when the boy took this flag from its staff, put it in his pocket, adjusted upon himself the accoutrements of the dead soldier, and fought gallantly in the ranks, until with 65 men and 3 officers he was taken prisoner. Concealing the flag under the lining of his coat, he kept it with him when taken to Richmond, and managed to bring it away unobserved when exchanged and sent home.

The flag is deposited by the lad's father, as an honorable memorial of the services of a patriotic son.

The other flags of the regiment were lost in the service.

COLORS OF THE 29TH REGIMENT N. Y. S. V.

(Three Flags.)

————— •• —————

This regiment was composed exclusively of Germans, and was organized in New York under Col. (now GENERAL) A. VON STEINWEHR. It was engaged in the 1st BATTLE OF BULL RUN, CROSS KEYS, WARRENTON SULPHUR SPRINGS, 2d BULL RUN, and CHANCELLORSVILLE, and upon the expiration of the two years' term of the regiment, its flags were placed for preservation in the State archives. The 29th was a part of the 1st Brigade, 2d Division, 11th Army Corps, and during the active period of the campaign of 1862, served under GENERAL FREMONT, in the Mountain Department, and in the Corps of GENERAL SIGEL, in the army of Virginia. It went to the field with 745 men, and returned with 559. During the two years, 33 men were killed fighting under these colors.

COLORS OF THE 32D REGIMENT N. Y. S. V.

(Two Flags.)

This regiment was originally intended to serve under Col. Baker of California, and for a time was called the "1st California Regiment." It was organized on Staten Island, from companies enlisted in Johnstown, Amsterdam, Ithaca, Tarrytown and New York city, and served as a part of the 3d Brigade, 1st Division, 6th Corps.

The National flag was presented to the 32d regiment, June 28th, 1861, by the lady of the Hon. Wm. Laimbier, Jr., of New York city; and the banner, by the city of New York, in the fall of 1861.

This regiment was engaged in the First Battle of Bull Run, West Point, Gaines' Mill, White Oak Swamp, Charles City Cross Roads, 2d Bull Run, Crampton Pass, Antietam, Fredericksburgh and Chancellorsville. During its

7

two years' term of service, the 32d regiment lost 34 killed, and 127 wounded in action Its colonel and major were mortally wounded at Crampton Pass, where the regiment charged on the enemy, and assisted in driving them up and over the mountain with heavy loss.

COLORS OF THE 34TH REGIMENT N. Y. S. V.

(One Flag.)

This regiment was organized at Albany, in May, 1861. Five of its companies were enrolled in Herkimer county, two in Steuben, one in Clinton, one in Essex, and one in West Troy, Albany county. It was mustered into the service of the United States, June 15th, and soon after being sent to the seat of war, was assigned to duty in Maryland on the upper Potomac.

It participated in the battle of BALL's BLUFF, the SEIGE OF YORKTOWN, battles of WEST POINT, FAIR OAKS, SEVEN PINES, PEACH ORCHARD STATION, SAVAGE'S STATION, WHITE OAK SWAMP, GLENDALE, MALVERN HILL, SOUTH MOUNTAIN, ANTIETAM, ASHBY'S GAP, and FREDERICKSBURGH.

The 34th was brigaded with the 1st Brigade, 2d Division, 2d Army Corps.

COLORS OF THE 37TH REGIMENT N. Y. S. V.

(Three Flags.)

This Regiment was raised in New York city, and was sometimes known as the "Irish Rifles."

Upon the expiration of its two years' term, it placed in the custody of the Bureau of Military Statistics, seven flags, including two guidons and two designation flags, together with all its papers and records.

The National flag that shows the greatest amount of service, was received by the regiment, when it arrived in Washington in July, 1861. In camp or in bivouack it was always before the regimental headquarters, and it was borne in the following battles: 1st BULL RUN (in reserve), WILLIAMSBURGH, FAIR OAKS, GLENDALE, MALVERN HILL, 2d BULL RUN, CHANTILLY, FREDERICKSBURGH and CHANCELLORSVILLE. It was also with the regiment in the SEIGE OF YORKTOWN, and in several skirmishes on the Occoquan, in front of York-town, Richmond, &c.

The Green banner was presented by the city of New York, in February, 1862, and was with the regiment in front of Fredericksburgh, and in the battle of Chancellorsville. It is inscribed with the names "Williamsburgh," "Fair Oaks," "Fredericksburgh," "Glendale," "Malvern Hill."

The new National flag, companion to the green banner, replaces on the original staff one that was lost at Chancellorsville. The flag was re-moved by LLOYD, the bearer, and wrapped around his body, as it was liable to be torn in passing through the tangled brush through which he was obliged to creep. This brave and intelligent soldier was killed, and his body was buried, without suspecting that the flag was wrapped around his person under his coat. Repeated efforts were made to find his grave, but without success.

COLORS OF THE 38TH REGIMENT N. Y. S. V.

(Two Flags.)

This regiment was organized in New York, under Colonel, now GENERAL J. H. HOBART WARD, and was known at that time as the "Second Regiment Scott Life Guard." These colors were presented by the citizens and the city of New York. The regiment before receiving them, was engaged in the FIRST BATTLE OF BULL RUN. It was subsequently in the SEIGE OF YORKTOWN, and the battles of WILLIAMSBURGH, FAIR OAKS, THE ORCHARD, GLENDALE. CHARLES CITY CROSS ROADS, MALVERN HILL, SECOND BULL RUN, CHANTILLY, FREDERICKSBURGH, CHANCELLORSVILLE and GETTYSBURGH.

COLORS OF THE 59TH REGIMENT N. Y. S. V.

(Three Flags.)

The regimental banner of this regiment was presented by Ex-Mayor KINGSLAND of New York, on behalf of citizens of that place, and the two other flags by the city of New York.

The regiment has been engaged in the following battles: MALVERN HILL, CHANTILLY, SOUTH MOUNTAIN, ANTIETAM, FIRST FREDERICKSBURGH, MAYRE'S HEIGHTS, THOROUGHFARE GAP, GETTYSBURGH, BRISTOW STATION and MINE RUN.

The loss at Antietam was very severe. Out of twenty-one officers and three hundred and sixty men which went into the fight, thirteen officers and two hundred and thirty men were killed, wounded or taken prisoners. Seven of the eight Color Guard were either killed or wounded, and the remaining one received and brought off the colors of a Pennsylvania regiment.

The top of the staff of one of the National flags was shattered by a shell bursting over it at the battle of Fredericksburgh, Dec. 13, 1862.

The flags were deposited by LIEUT. COL. H. P. RUGG, with two guidons received from the city of New York.

COLORS OF THE 61ST REGIMENT N. Y. S. V.

(One Flag.)

This regiment was organized in New York in the fall of 1861, under the name of the "Clinton Life Guards."

This flag was presented by the city of New York, and was used as a parade flag until the Peninsular campaign. It was laid aside until the spring of 1863, when it was again used through the season as a regimental flag. It was carried through the battles of CHANCELLORSVILLE, GETTYS-BURGH, AUBURN, BRISTOW STATION, and MINE RUN.

At Gettysburgh, the Color Bearer and two of the guard were severely wounded. The loss here was one officer killed and five wounded, and sixty-eight enlisted men killed and wounded. This flag is sent to the State archives for preservation, by COL. NELSON A. MILES.

8

While on the Peninsula, this regiment was engaged in the battles of YORKTOWN, FAIR OAKS, PEACH ORCHARD, SAVAGE'S STATION, WHITE OAK SWAMP, and CHARLES CITY CROSS ROADS, and subsequently at ANTIETAM, CHARLESTOWN, SNICKER'S GAP and FREDERICKSBURGH. The flag under which the regiment fought their battles, was presented at the last session of the Legislature.

COLORS OF THE 64TH REGIMENT N. Y. S. V.

(One Flag.)

———— •◆• ————

This regiment was enlisted chiefly in Cattaraugus, Allegany and Tompkins counties. It was engaged in the SEIGE OF YORKTOWN and in the battles of FAIR OAKS, GAINES' MILL, PEACH ORCHARD, SAVAGE'S STATION, WHITE OAK SWAMP, MALVERN HILL, ANTIETAM, FREDERICKSBURGH, CHANCELLORSVILLE and GETTYSBURGH. It was also engaged in several skirmishes, the most important of which were at SOUTH MOUNTAIN, CHARLESTOWN, VA., and SNICKER'S GAP.

At Gettysburgh, on the 2d of July, 1863, this flag was carried by Chauncey McKoon of Company B, who was severely wounded in the thigh. It was then taken by Edmund Stone, Company D, who was killed. It was then raised by Sergeant Blackmore, who carried it through the remainder of the battle, and brought it off safe.

It is transmitted to the Bureau of Military Statistics by COL. D. G. BINGHAM, the present Colonel.

COLORS OF THE 75TH REGIMENT N. Y. S. V.

(One Flag.)

———— •• ————

This regiment was organized at Auburn, Nov. 14, 1861, and left the State on the 30th of that month, receiving this flag at the hands of ladies of Auburn before its departure.

The 75th served several months at Key West and Pensacola, and formed a part of the expedition of GENERAL BANKS. It was engaged in the three battles before PORT HUDSON, May 25th, May 27th, and June 14th, 1863, and has since been engaged in important services in Louisiana.

The colors were transmitted to the Bureau of Military Statistics, by COL. ROBERT B. MERRITT, the present commandant.

COLORS OF THE 76TH REGIMENT N. Y. S. V.

(One Flag.)

----◆◆----

This regiment was organized in Cortland county, and left the State in January, 1862. In the ensuing campaign it was brigaded with the 2d Brigade, 1st Division, 1st Army Corps, and shared the fortunes of the army under Generals POPE and McCLELLAN, in the campaign of Virginia and Maryland, participating in the battles of RAPPAHANNOCK STATION, WARRENTON SULPHUR SPRINGS, GAINESVILLE, SECOND BULL RUN, SOUTH MOUNTAIN, ANTIETAM and UPPERVILLE. It served under General BURNSIDE at the battle of FREDE-RICKSBURGH; under General HOOKER during four days marching and fighting at CHANCELLORSVILLE; and under General MEADE at GETTYSBURGH and MINE RUN.

This flag was presented to the regiment on the

steps of the Capitol in Albany, upon its departure for the field, by Mrs. CAMPBELL of York Mills, Oneida county, with public ceremonies, and was carried until December, 1863. It received fifteen musket balls and one twelve pound shot through it in action. The Color Bearer, Sergeant Champ, was killed at South Mountain. At Gettysburgh the Color Bearer was wounded just as the regiment was falling back, and came near being captured, but was rescued by private John Stephens of Company H, who left the ranks under the fire of the enemy, and recovered the flag in safety. He was promoted to a Sergeant for his gallantry on that occasion.

The flag is transmitted to the Bureau of Military Statistics by Captain A. L. SWAN, of Company H, of the 76th regiment.

COLORS OF THE 77TH REGIMENT N. Y. S. V.

(One Flag.)

This regiment was organized in Saratoga county, and while forming, was known as the "Bemis Heights Regiment." This flag was presented November 29, 1861, by citizens of Saratoga county, resident in New York city. It has been carried in the battle of LEE's MILLS, the SEIGE OF YORKTOWN, battles of MECHANICSVILLE, GOLDEN'S FARM, GARNET'S HILL, WHITE OAK SWAMP, CRAMPTON PASS, ANTIETAM, FREDERICKSBURGH, MAYRES' HEIGHTS and GETTYSBURGH. The Bearers were Sergeant Isaac Bemis, and afterwards Corporal Michael McWilliams. In the charge up Mayres' Heights, one of the Color Guard was killed, and the flag was torn into shreds by a shell.

The Guide colors (one of which is attached),

were presented at the same time and place, have been used during the same period. That on the right of the line was crimson, and that on the left, blue.

COLORS OF THE 20TH N. Y. STATE MILITIA.

"80TH N. Y. S. VOLUNTEERS."

(One Flag.)

This regiment, sometimes known as the "Ulster Guard," went to the field as a militia regiment, under Col. Geo. W. Pratt, for a term of three months, a few days after the beginning of the war.

Upon its return it was re-organized for three years, and it has recently re-enlisted for the war.

This regiment was in the battles of Rappahannock Station, Warrenton Springs, Groveton, 2d Bull Run (where Colonel Pratt was mortally wounded), Chantilly, South Mountain, Antietam, Fredericksburgh, Chancellorsville and Gettysburgh.

The regiment lost 35 killed and 232 wounded in the campaign of 1862, while fighting under these colors.

COLORS OF THE 91ST REGIMENT N. Y. S. V.

(One Flag.)

Upon the departure of the 91st from Albany for Key West, in December, 1861, it received a National flag, of which the one here exhibited is a part. The regiment served for some time at Pensacola, and subsequently under Gen. BANKS in Louisiana.

It was engaged at IRISH BEND, VERMILLION, BAYOU, and the three battles before PORT HUDSON, of May 25th and 27th, and June 14th, 1863. In one of these the flag was torn in two, and this portion was brought into a hospital by one of the Color Guard, who was wounded. The part that remained on the lance is still with the regiment, and in due time the two will be re-united.

This flag is presented through Col. HARCOURT of Albany, by whom it was originally presented to the regiment.

COLORS OF THE 96TH REGIMENT N. Y. S. V.

(One Flag.)

This regiment was organized at Plattsburgh under Col. FAIRMAN. It served in the SEIGE OF YORKTOWN, and the battles of WILLIAMSBURGH, SEVEN PINES, FAIR OAKS, CHICKAHOMINY SWAMP, WHITE OAK SWAMP, RAIL ROAD BRIDGE, BOTTOM BRIDGE, LONG'S BRIDGE, JONES' FORD, CHARLES CITY CROSS ROADS, HARRISON'S POINT, BLACK WATER and KINSTON.

Col. CHARLES O. GRAY succeeded to the command of the regiment, and was killed in action, Dec. 14, 1862, in the act of planting his colors on the enemy's position, on the bridge over the Neuse River, at Kinston, N. C.

This regiment has re-enlisted with General LEDLIE's Veteran Brigade, and is now serving in the Department of North Carolina.

COLORS OF THE 97TH REGIMENT N. Y. S. V.

(One Flag.)

———— ◆◇ ————

This regiment was organized at Boonville, and was made up by enlistments in Oneida, Lewis and Herkimer counties. These colors were presented to the regiment by the ladies of Boonville, and have been carried in the battles of CEDAR MOUNTAIN, RAPPAHANNOCK STATION, THOROUGHFARE GAP, 2d BULL RUN, CHANTILLY, SOUTH MOUNTAIN, ANTIETAM, FREDERICKSBURGH, CHANCELLORSVILLE and GETTYSBURGH.

A portion of this regiment has re-enlisted for the war, and the record of its services are of the most honorable character. Its numbers, at one time greatly reduced by casualties, have been increased by conscripts and substitutes, to a full and efficient regiment.

COLORS OF THE 104TH REGIMENT N. Y. S. V.

(One Flag.)

This banner was presented to the 104th regiment (Wadsworth Guard), by Gen. JAMES S. WADSWORTH, in April, 1862, and it was carried through the campaign of 1862, under General POPE and McCLELLAN; and in 1863 on the march into Maryland and Pennsylvania.

This regiment was under an active cannonade on the evening following the battle of CEDAR MOUNTAIN, in the three days' battle on the RAPPAHANNOCK, and at the battles of THOROUGHFARE GAP, SECOND BULL RUN, SOUTH MOUNTAIN, ANTIETAM, FREDERICKSBURGH, CHANCELLORSVILLE and GETTYSBURGH, besides in numerous skirmishes.

One of the Bearers was severely wounded at South Mountain, and another at Antietam. At Gettysburgh, seven of the Sergeants and Color Guard were killed or wounded in sustaining them, and the Corporal who took the National flag being in danger of capture, tore the flag from the staff and stamped it into the ground to conceal it from the enemy's notice. This flag was barely saved by great vigilance.

The 104th has sustained an honorable reputation, and is still in the service. The flag is sent by Lieut. Col. STRONG, for preservation in the State archives.

The 104th regiment was organized at Geneseo, and made up of volunteers enlisted in Livingston county, with the exception of three companies from Troy, that were consolidated before leaving the State.

COLORS OF THE 130TH REGIMENT N. Y. S. V.

(One Flag.)

This regiment was organized by the Senatorial Committee of the 30th District, at Portage, and was recruited in Livingston, Wyoming and Allegany counties. In the autumn of 1862, it was sent to Fortress Monroe, and was engaged in the operations near Suffolk, as a part of the Seventh Army Corps. On the 11th day of August, 1863, this regiment was changed to the 19th N. Y. Cavalry, and since September, 10th, 1863, it has been known as the First Regiment of Dragoons, New York State Volunteers. These colors were borne by the regiment only during its services as an Infantry organization.

COLORS OF THE 146TH REGIMENT N. Y. S. V.

(One Flag.)

———— •◆• ————

This regiment was organized at Rome, under the direction of the Senatorial Committee of the 19th District, and left the State September 27, 1862. It was assigned to the 3d Brigade, 2d Division, 5th Army Corps, and fought at FREDE-RICKSBURGH, CHANCELLORSVILLE and GETTYSBURGH, as a part of the 3d Brigade, 2d Division, 5th Corps.

COLORS OF THE 177TH REGIMENT N. Y. S. V.

(Two Flags.)

The 10th regiment National Guards was organized for a nine months' term of service, under the name of the "177th Volunteers," at Albany, in November, 1862, and sent with Gen. Banks' Expedition to the Department of the Gulf.

It was attached to the 3d Brigade, 2d Division, 19th Corps, and served in two campaigns upon the Amite River, and through the entire Seige of Port Hudson, taking part in the battles of May 27 and June 14, 1863.

The regiment returned in August, 1863, by way of the Mississippi River, the route originally promised by General Banks to the troops of his Expedition.

The National flag here presented, was received by the regiment while stationed at Bonne Carrie, La., from Mrs. Merrihew, the wife of an officer of the regiment.

COLORS

OF THE

3D N. Y. STATE ARTILLERY REGIMENT,

FORMERLY THE 19TH REGIMENT OF INFANTRY.

(One Flag.)

————— ◆◆ —————

This regiment entered the field in the summer of 1861, and on the 11th of December of that year, was changed to Artillery. Four companies were added, and in April it was sent to Newbern, N. C. The banner here exhibited is inscribed by authority with the names of battles in which it has been engaged: LOVETTSVILLE, FORT MACON, WASHINGTON, N. C., SOUTH WEST CREEK, KINSTON, WHITEHALL, GOLDSBOROUGH, NEWBERN, and SEIGE OF WASHINGTON. The greater part of this regiment have re-enlisted with General LEDLIE's Veteran Brigade.

COLORS

OF THE

7TH N. Y. STATE INDEPENDENT BATTERY.

(One Flag.)

This battery was raised in Newburgh and Cornwall, under Captain PETER C. REGAN, and originally formed a part of the "Tenth Legion," or 56th regiment N. Y. Volunteers.

Upon entering the field it was detached and made an Independent Battery.

It served on the Peninsula, and subsequently with the 7th Army Corps, in Southeastern Virginia. The guidon was struck by a shell at the battle of Fair Oaks.

COLORS

OF THE

IITH N. Y. STATE INDEPENDENT BATTERY.

(Three Flags.)

The flag, banner and guidon exhibited, belonged to the Eleventh N. Y. Independent Battery, sometimes called the "Havelock Battery," which was raised in Albany, under the auspices of the Young Men's Christian Association.

After serving several months as heavy artillery, it was sent to the field, and the guidon is inscribed by authority with the names of the following battles, in which it has participated: MANASSAS, CHANTILLY, MINE RUN, GETTYSBURGH, BRISTOW STATION, CHANCELLORSVILLE, RAPPAHANNOCK and FREDERICKSBURGH.

HISTORY OF THE NATIONAL FLAG.

BY ALFRED B. STREET.

The most interesting incident connected with the battle of Saratoga was the unfurling, for the first time, the Stars and Stripes at the surrender of Burgoyne.

Bunker Hill was fought under a red flag, bearing the motto, "Come if you dare!" but on the 14th of June, 1777, the Continental Congress resolved "That the flag of the thirteen United States be thirteen stripes, alternate red and white, and that the Union be thirteen stars, white on a blue field, representing a new constellation."

This was made public on the 3d of September following. Previous to this our National banner was the Union flag, combining the crosses of St. George and St. Andrew (taken from the English banner) with thirteen stripes, alternate red and white. The banner of St. Patrick (Ireland's emblem) was not combined with the crosses of St. George and St. Andrew in the Standard of Great Britain until 1801, the year of the union with Ireland.

The stars of the new flag represented the new constellation of States, the idea taken from the constellation Lyra, which signifies harmony. The blue of the field was taken from the Covenanters' banner in Scotland, likewise significant of the league and covenant of the United Colonies against oppression, and incidentally involving vigilance, perseverance and justice. The stars were disposed in a circle, symbolizing the perpetuity of the Union, the circle being the sign of eternity. The thirteen stripes showed, with the stars, the number of the United Colonies, and denoted the subordination of the States to, and their dependence upon the Union, as well as equality among themselves. The whole was a blending of the various flags previous to the Union flag, viz: the red flags of the army and white ones of the floating batteries — the germ of our navy. The red color, also, which in Roman days was the signal of defiance, denoted daring, and the white purity.

By the United States law of January 13, 1794, it was enacted " that, from and after the first of May, 1795, the flag of the United States shall be fifteen stripes, alternate red and white, and " that the Union be fifteen stars, white in a blue field." This was our National flag during the war of 1812.

On the 4th of April, 1818, Congress altered the flag, by directing a return to the thirteen stripes, as follows:

" Be it enacted, etc., That from and after the 4th day of July next, the flag of the United States be thirteen horizontal stripes, alternate red and white ; that the Union be twenty stars, white, in a blue field.

" And be it further enacted, That, on the admission of a new State into the Union, one star be added to the union of the flag; and that such addition shall take effect on the 4th day of July next succeeding such admission."

The return to the thirteen stripes was by

reason of the anticipation that the addition of a stripe on the admission of each State would make the flag too unwieldy. The old number of stripes also perpetuated the original number of States of the Union, while the addition of the stars showed the Union in its existing state.

The flag planted by our troops in the city of Mexico, at the conclusion of the Mexican war, bore thirty stars.

The size of the flag for the army is six feet six inches in length, by six feet in width, with seven red and six white stripes. The first seven stripes (four red and three white) bound the square of the blue field for the stars, the stripes extending from the extremity of the field to the end of the flag. The eighth stripe is white, extending partly at the base of the field. The number of stars is thirty-five.

What eloquence do the Stars and Stripes breathe, when their full significance is known! A new constellation; union; perpetuity; a covenant against oppression; equality; subordination; courage; purity.

11

Success to the Flag of our Nation !
  Its folds all around us be spread !
Emblazoned with deeds of the valiant,
  And sacred with names of the dead !
Its stars are the symbol of Union,
  In Union they ever shall wave !
Its white is the emblem of honor !
  Its red is the blood of the brave.

Success to the Flag of our Nation !
  Let it stream o'er the land and the sea !
The shades of our heroes are round it,
  Beneath it, the ranks of the Free.
Let us swear we will ever defend it
  In the trials to come, as of yore,
Lift it high, a broad beacon of Freedom
  To the world, until Time is no more !

www.ingramcontent.com/pod-product-compliance
Lightning Source LLC
Chambersburg PA
CBHW021423090426
42742CB00009B/1234